PRESENTED TO

FROM

DATE

Dr. JAMES DOBSON

Life on the Edge

W PUBLISHING GROUP

www.wpublishinggroup.com

A Division of Thomas Nelson, Inc.
www.ThomasNelson.com

Compiled and edited by Nancy Guthrie

All text originally appeared in *Life on the Edge* by James Dobson © 1995 by James Dobson.

Unless otherwise indicated, Scripture quotations used in this book are from
The Holy Bible, New International Version (NIV). Copyright © 1973, 1978, 1984
International Bible Society. Used by permission of Zondervan Bible Publishers.

Other references are from the following sources:
The King James Version of the Bible (KJV). The Living Bible (TLB),
copyright 1971 by Tyndale House Publishers. Wheaton, Ill. Used by permission.
The New King James Version (NKJV). Copyright © 1979, 1980, 1982, 1990,
Thomas Nelson, Inc., Publisher. The New Testament in Modern English (PHILLIPS) by
J. B. Phillips; published by The Macmillan Company. © 1958, 1960, 1972 by J. B. Phillips.

ISBN 0-8499-1629-1

Printed in the United States of America
02 03 04 RRD 9 8 7 6 5 4 3

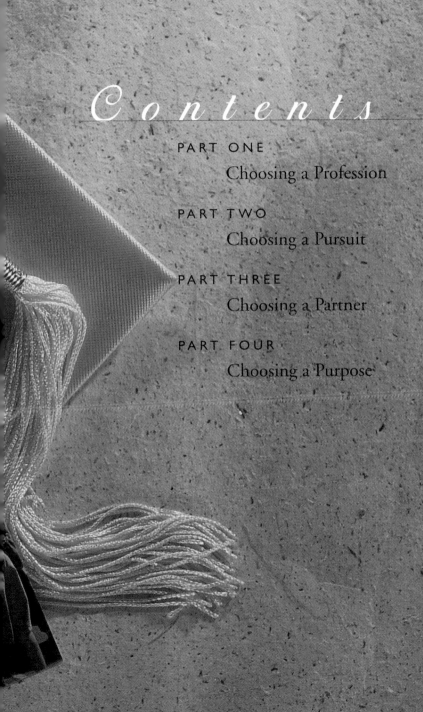

Contents

Congratulations,
GRADUATE

YOU'VE DONE IT.

You've worked hard and accomplished

a great deal.

But there is still so much ahead—

still so much ahead to explore as you

begin to build your life to come.

Your next ten years, which we will call the "critical decade," will pose hundreds of important questions for which secure answers may be slow in coming. I struggled with many of them when I was in college, such as, What will I do with my life? What kind of woman should I marry? Where will I find her? Will our love last a lifetime? What are my strengths and weaknesses? Should I plan to attend graduate school? Can I qualify for admission? Am I talented enough to make it professionally? And what about God? Where does He fit into my plans, and how can I know His will?

It is so important to pause and think through some basic issues while you are young, before the pressures of job and family become distracting. There are several eternal questions everyone must deal with eventually. You will benefit, I think, from doing that work now.

Over the next several years, you will be transformed from a kid who's still living at home and eating at your parents' table, to a full-fledged adult who should be earning a living and taking complete charge of your life. Most of the decisions that will shape the next fifty years will be made in the near future, including the choice of an occupation, perhaps the decision to marry, and the establishment of values and principles by which life will be governed.

Let's consider these important choices together in the pages that follow so that graduation will only be the beginning of a very meaningful future.

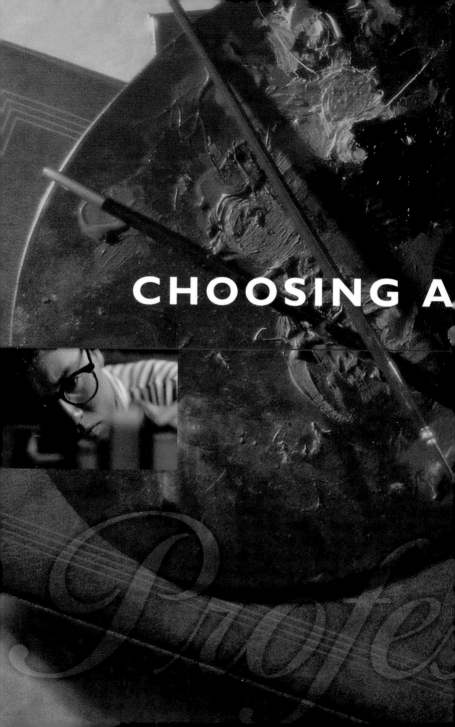

CHOOSING A

PROFESSION

One of the most important decisions to be made in the next few years will focus on a life's work—an occupation—or a skill you hope to develop. That choice is often extremely difficult. How can you predict what you'll want to be doing when you're forty or fifty or sixty years old? You're obligated to guess, based on very limited information. You may not even know what the work is really like, yet you enroll yourself in a lengthy academic program to train for it.

The decisions you make under those circumstances may lock you into something you will later hate. And there are social pressures that influence your choices. For example, many young women secretly want to be wives and mothers, but are afraid to admit it in today's "liberated" society. Furthermore, how can a girl plan to do something that requires the participation of another person—a husband who will be worthy of loving her and living with her for the rest of her life? Marriage may or may not be in the picture for her. Yes, there's plenty to consider in this critical decade.

I feel very fortunate to have stumbled into a profession when I was young that I have been able to do reasonably well. If I had been born in Jesus' time and had been required to earn a living with my hands, perhaps in carpentry or stonemasonry, I would have probably starved to death. I can see myself sitting outside the temple in Jerusalem with a sign that read, "Will work for food." Craftsmanship is just not in my nature. I earned my only high school D in woodworking class, and that was a gift from my teacher, Mr. Peterson. I spent an entire semester trying to make a box in which to store shoeshine stuff. What a waste! At least that experience helped me rule out a few occupational possibilities. Carpentry and cabinetry were two of them.

THINGS TO CONSIDER WHEN CHOOSING A PROFESSION

You'll have to rule some things in and out, too. Indeed, to make an informed decision about a profession, you'll need to get six essential components together, as follows:

1. It must be something you genuinely like to do. This choice requires you to identify your own strengths, weaknesses, and interests. (Some excellent psychometric tests are available to help with this need.)

2. It must be something you have the ability to do. You might want to be an attorney but lack the talent to do the academic work and pass the bar examination.

3. It must be something you can earn a living by doing. You might want to be an artist, but if people don't buy your paintings, you could starve while sitting at your easel.

4. It must be something you are permitted to do. You might make a wonderful physician and could handle the training but can't gain entrance to medical school. I went through a Ph.D. program in graduate school with a fellow student who was washed out after seven years of

classwork. He made it to the last big exam before his professors told him, "You're out."

5. It must be something that brings cultural affirmation. In other words, most people need to feel some measure of respect from their contemporaries for what they do. This is one reason women have found it difficult to stay home and raise their children.

6. Most importantly for the genuine believer, it must be something that you feel God approves of. How do you determine the will of God about so personal a decision? That is a critical matter we'll discuss presently.

What makes it so tough to choose an occupation is that all six of these requirements must be met at the same time. If you get five of them down but you don't like what you have selected, you're in trouble. If you get five together but are rejected by the required professional

A person doesn't go to college just to prepare for a line of work—or at least, that shouldn't be the reason for being there. The purpose for getting a college education is to broaden your world and enrich your intellectual life. Whether or not it leads to a career is not the point. Nothing invested in the cultivation of your own mind is ever really wasted. If you have the desire to learn and the opportunity to go to school, I think you should reach for it. Your career plans can be finalized later.

schools, you are blocked. If you get five lined up but you can't earn a living at the job of your choice, the system fails. Every link in the chain must connect.

Given this challenge, it isn't surprising that so many young people flounder during the critical decade. They become immobilized for years not knowing what to do next. They sit around their parents' house plunking on a guitar and waiting for a dish to rattle in the kitchen.

Young adults in this situation remind me of rockets sitting on the launch pad. Their engines are roaring and belching smoke and fire, but nothing moves. The spacecraft was made to blast its way through the stratosphere, but there it sits as if bolted to the pad. I've met many men and women in their early twenties whose rockets just would not lift them off the ground. And yes, I've known a few whose engines blew up and scattered the debris of broken dreams all over the launch pad.

The mission sometimes fails because an individual refuses to include God in his lofty plans. The psalmist wrote, "Except the LORD build the house, they labour in vain that build it: except the LORD keep the city, the watchman waketh but in vain" (PS. 127:1 KJV). Those words offer incredible meaning for those of you who are just getting started in life. Whatever you try to do, whether it is to build or defend, will be useless if you do it in your own strength. That may sound very

The mission of choosing an occupation sometimes fails because an individual refuses to include God in his lofty plans.

old-fashioned, but I promise you it is true. Furthermore, the Lord will not settle for second place in your life.

LESSONS FROM MY FATHER

My father thought he would be an exception to that principle. He had his life laid out, and he needed no help from God or anyone else in fulfilling it. From his earliest childhood, Dad knew he wanted to be a great artist. Even before kindergarten, he told his family he intended to draw and paint when he grew up. This passion was not simply a choice he had made. It was in his blood. All through childhood and his teen years, he never wavered from this desire to become another Rembrandt or Michelangelo. While his five brothers were uncertain about what they wanted to be, this youngest among them was chasing a lofty dream.

Then one day as he walked along a street during his sixteenth year, he seemed to hear the Lord speaking to

him. It was not an audible voice, of course. But deep within his being he knew he had been addressed by the Almighty. It was a simple message that conveyed this thought: I want you to set aside your great ambition to be an artist and prepare for a life of service in the ministry.

My father was terrified by the experience. He replied, "No! No, Lord. You know I have my plans all made and art is my consuming interest." He quickly argued down the impression and convinced himself that his mind had deceived him. But when he got it all resolved and laid to rest, it would reappear. Month after month, the nagging thought reverberated in his mind that God was asking—no, demanding—that he abandon his dream and become a preacher. It proved to be one of the greatest struggles of his life, but he shared it with no one.

For two years this inner battle went on. Then toward the end of his senior year in high school, the time came for him to select a college to attend in the fall. His father told him to pick out any school in the country and he would send him there. But what was he to do? If he yielded to the voice within, he would have to attend a college that would begin preparing him for the ministry. But if he followed his dream, he would go to art school. Would he obey God, or would he have his own way? It was a terrible dilemma.

One morning a few weeks before graduation, he got out of bed to prepare for school. But the minute his feet touched the floor, my father heard the voice again. It was as if the Lord said, Today you will have to make up your mind. He wrestled with that issue all day at school but still shared his turmoil with no one. After his last class in midafternoon, he came home to an empty house. He paced back and forth in the living room, praying and struggling with this unrelenting demand of God. Finally, in an act of defiance, he suddenly turned his face upward and said, "It's too great a price, and I won't pay it!"

My father later described that moment as the most terrible experience of his life. He said the Spirit of the Lord seemed to leave him as one person would walk away from another. He was still shaken and pale when his mother came home a

It was a simple message: Set aside your great ambition to be an artist and prepare for a life of service in the ministry.

few minutes later. She could see his distress, and she asked him what was wrong.

"You won't understand this, Mom," he said, "but God has been asking me to give up my plans to be an artist. He wants me to become a minister. I don't want to do it. And I won't do it. I've just said no to Him, and He's gone."

My grandmother was a very righteous woman who could always touch the heart of God in her prayers. She said, "Oh, Honey, you're just emotional. Let's pray about it."

They got down on their knees, and my grandmother began talking to the Lord about her son. Then she stopped in midsentence. "I don't understand it," she said. "Something is wrong."

"You don't understand it," said my father, "but I do. I've just refused to obey God, and He's gone."

It would be seven long years before my father would hear the voice of the Lord again. You see, his love of art had become his god. It mattered more to him than anything on earth and even outranked his relationship with the Father. That's what was going on in his heart. There was nothing sinful or immoral in his love of art. The problem was that God had no place in it.

In the next few days, my father chose the Art Institute of Pittsburgh (AIP), one of the best art schools in the country. He enrolled there in the fall, and his professors immediately recognized his unusual talent. Indeed, when he graduated, he was honored as the most gifted student in his class. But as he was walking down the aisle to the platform where a big NUMBER ONE banner had been draped on his paintings, the Scripture again came into his mind: "Except the LORD build the house, they labour in vain that build it."

One of the secrets of successful living is found in the word balance, referring to the avoidance of harmful extremes. We need food, but we should not overeat. We should work, but not make work our only activity. We should play, but not let play rule us. Throughout life, it will be important to find the safety of the middle ground rather than the imbalance of the extremes.

My father graduated and went out to begin his great career in the field of art. Unfortunately, the Great Depression was under way in the United States and in most countries around the world. That was a scary time in American history when huge numbers of people were out of work. Businesses failed, banks closed, and opportunities were few and far between. My dad was one of the millions who couldn't find a job of any type— much less one in his chosen profession. He was finally hired at a Texaco service station to pump gas and wipe the windshields of cars. It was pretty humbling for a man who wanted to be another Leonardo da Vinci.

Here is the most incredible part of the

story. Right at that moment when my dad was desperate for a career break, the president of the Art Institute of Pittsburgh wrote him a letter and offered him a job as an instructor at the unbelievable salary of three hundred dollars per month! It was precisely what he had dreamed about since childhood. But somehow that letter became lost on the president's desk. The man later found and mailed it with another note saying he had wondered why my dad hadn't even done him the courtesy of responding to his offer. But by the time the second letter came, my father had grown sick of himself and his lofty plans. He had found a place of prayer and yielded himself completely to the call of God on his life. So by the time the job offer

came, he wrote back to say, "Thanks, but I'm no longer interested."

WHEN EVERYTHING
TURNS ON ONE DECISION

My dad's future, and undoubtedly mine, hung in the balance at that critical juncture. If he had received the original offer from the president of AIP, he would have been launched on a career that was obviously out of the will of God. Who knows how his life would have changed if he had "labored in vain" in the wrong vineyard? What prevented him from making the mistake of his life? Well, my grandmother was out there praying for him every day, asking the Lord to draw her youngest son back to Himself. I believe God answered her prayers by interfering with the delivery of the letter on which everything seemed to depend.

Does it seem cruel of the Lord to deprive this young man of the one thing he most wanted? Good question! Why would God give him remarkable ability and then prevent him from using it? Well, as is always the case in His dealings with us, the Lord had my father's best interests at heart. And He took nothing away from him.

As soon as my dad yielded to the will of the Lord, his art was given back to him. He then used his talent in ministerial work all his life, and when he died he was chairman of the art department at a Christian college. He left beautiful paintings and sculptures all over the United States. More importantly, thousands of people came to know Jesus Christ through the preaching ministry of my

As soon as my dad yielded to the will of the Lord, his art was given back to him.

father. They will be in heaven because of the calling that was on his life.

So the terrible struggle that occurred in my father's teen years was not a cruel manipulation. It was a vitally important test of his commitment—a challenge to put God in first place. And because he passed that test, I am here writing to you today!

Jesus Christ will ask you to put Him in first place, too. He will be Lord of all, or not Lord at all. That does not mean you will be required to become a minister. Your calling will be unique. But I am certain that anything done selfishly and independent of His purposes will not satisfy you and will ultimately be done "in vain."

Your life is before you.

Be careful of the choices you make now

that you could regret later. This regret is the subject

of an old poem whose author has been forgotten.

I hope you'll never have reason to apply it to yourself.

Across the fields of yesterday,

He sometimes comes to me

A little lad just back from play—

The boy I used to be.

He looks at me so wistfully

When once he's crept within;

It is as if he hoped to see

The man I might have been.

CHOOSING A

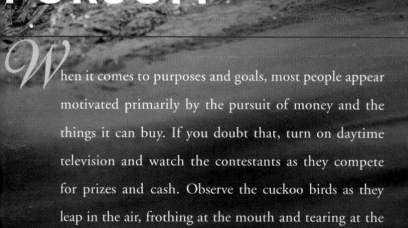

PURSUIT

*W*hen it comes to purposes and goals, most people appear motivated primarily by the pursuit of money and the things it can buy. If you doubt that, turn on daytime television and watch the contestants as they compete for prizes and cash. Observe the cuckoo birds as they leap in the air, frothing at the mouth and tearing at the clothes of the host. Notice that their eyes are dilated and their ears are bright pink. It's a condition known as game-show greed, and it renders its victims incapable of rational judgment.

Yes, BETTY MOLINO,
YOU have won a NEW WASHING MACHINE,
a year's supply of CHEWY CANDY BARS,
and this marvelous new doll, WANDA WEE-WEE,
that actually soaks your daughter's lap!
CONGRATULATIONS, BETTY,
and thanks for playing "GRAB BAG"
(frantic applause).

How do I know so much about game-show greed? Because I've been there! Back in 1967, my lovely wife managed to drag me to the *Let's Make a Deal* show, which was the rage at that time. Shirley put toy birds all over her head and blouse, and I carried a dumb sign that said, "My wife is for the birds." Really funny, huh?

It was good enough to get the host, Monty Hall, to choose us as lucky contestants. The producers placed us in the two front seats near the cameras but began the program by "dealing" with other suckers.

I kept thinking as I sat there in contestants' row, *What in the world am I doing here holding this stupid sign?* I couldn't have been more skeptical about the proposition. Finally, Monty called our names, and the cameras zoomed in.

> *"Here behind door number one is . . .*
> *(a curtain opens) . . . A NEEEEW CAAR!!"*
> *(The audience goes crazy with excitement.)*

Suddenly, I was gripped by a spasm in the pit of my stomach. My mouth watered profusely, and my heart began knocking on the sides of my chest. There on that stage was the car of my dreams—a brand-new Camaro. Desire came charging up my throat and stuck in the region of my Adam's apple. My breathing became irregular and shallow, which was another unmistakable clue that I had been struck by game-show greed.

To understand this reaction, you would have to know that I have owned several of the worst cars in automotive history. Throughout my college years I drove a 1949 Mercury convertible (I called it Ol' Red) that had power seats, power windows, power top, power everything—but no power to run them. I put the windows up in the winter and down in the summer. There they remained, despite fluctuating temperatures. Shirley, who was then my girlfriend, must have loved me tremendously to have put up with that car. She hated it! The front seat had a spring with a bad temper that tore her clothes and punctured her skin. Nor did Ol' Red always choose to run. Every few days, Shirley and I would take this junk heap out for a push.

WHY I WANTED THAT NEW CAR

The crowning blow occurred shortly after our graduation from college. We were invited to appear for important job interviews, and we put on our Sunday best for the occasion. There we were, suit and tie, heels and hose, going sixty miles an hour down the road in Ol' Red, when the convertible top suddenly blew off. Strings and dust flapped us in the face as the canvas waved behind the car like Superman's cape. The ribs of the top protruded above our heads, reminiscent of undersized roll-over bars. It was very embarrassing. And can you believe that Shirley got mad at me for letting that happen? She crouched on the floorboard, blaming me for driving such a beat-up car. It is a miracle that our relationship survived that emotional afternoon.

Although Ol' Red had been put to sleep long before our appearance on *Let's Make a Deal,* I still had never owned a new car. Every available dollar had been allocated for

Whatever a person hungers for, Satan will appear to offer in exchange for a spiritual compromise.

tuition in graduate school. I had finished my Ph.D. just two months earlier.

This explains my reaction to the beautiful automobile behind door number one.

"All you have to do to win the car," said Monty, "is tell us the prices of four items."

Shirley and I guessed the first three but blew it on number four. "Sorry," said Monty. "You've been zonked. But here, take a vacuum cleaner and three dollars. And thanks for playing *Let's Make a Deal!*"

Shirley and I were just sick. On the way home we talked about how our emotions had been manipulated in that situation. We both experienced incredible greed, and the feeling was not comfortable. I have since learned a very valuable lesson about lust and how it operates in a spiritual context. It has been my observation that whatever a person hungers for, Satan will appear to offer in exchange for a spiritual compromise. In my case, a new automobile was the perfect enticement to unleash my greed. If illicit sex is your desire, it will eventually be made available. Don't be surprised when you are beckoned by a willing partner.

If your passion is for fame or power, that object of lust will be promised (even if never delivered).

Remember that Jesus was offered bread following His forty-day fast in the wilderness. He was promised power and glory after He had been contemplating

Satan will attempt to offer you whatever you hunger for, whether it be money, power, sex, or prestige. But Jesus said, "Blessed are those who hunger and thirst for righteousness" (MATT. 5:6).

His upcoming road to the cross. My point is that Satan uses our keenest appetites to tempt us.

WATCH OUT! TEMPTATION AHEAD!

Likewise, if you hunger and thirst for great wealth— beware! You are in a very precarious position. If you doubt it, look at 1 Timothy 6:9, which says, "People who want to get rich fall into temptation and a trap and into many foolish and harmful desires that plunge men into ruin and destruction." What incredible insight into the nature of mankind. If you watch people who care passionately about money, you'll observe that many of them are suckers for wild-eyed schemes and shady deals. They are always on the verge of a bonanza that seems to slip through their fingers. Instead of getting rich, they just get taken.

Not only are there pitfalls for those who seek riches, but the few who acquire them are in for a disappointment. They quickly learn that wealth will not satisfy their need for significance. No amount of money will do that.

A popular bumper sticker reads, "He who dies with the most toys, wins." It's a lie. It should read, "He who dies with the most toys, dies anyway." I hope you will believe me when I say that a lifetime invested in the accumulation of things will have been wasted. There has to be a better reason for living than that.

MONEY: JESUS' MOST TALKED-ABOUT TOPIC

Jesus' own teachings have great relevance for us at this point. Have you ever wondered what topic He talked about more often than any other? Was it heaven, hell, sin, repentance, love, or His second coming? No, it was money, and most of what He said came in the form of a warning. This caution about possessions and riches appeared throughout Jesus' teachings. Here are a few passages just from one of the four Gospels, the Book of Luke:

Jesus said to a crowd of His followers, "But woe to you who are rich, for you have already received your comfort" (LUKE 6:24).

He also said, "Watch out! Be on your guard against all kinds of greed; a man's life does not consist in the abundance of his possessions" (LUKE 12:15).

Jesus told a parable about a rich fool who had no need of God. The man believed he had many years to live and said to himself, "'You have plenty of good things laid up for many years. Take life easy; eat, drink and be merry.' But God said to him, 'You fool! This very night your life will be demanded from you. Then who will get what you have prepared for yourself?'" Jesus ended the parable with this sober warning, "This is how it will be with anyone who stores up things for himself but is not rich toward God" (LUKE 12:19–21).

Jesus later visited the home of a prominent Pharisee and said to His host, "When you give a luncheon or dinner, do not invite your friends, your brothers or relatives, or your rich neighbors; if you do, they may invite you back and so you will be repaid. But when you give a banquet, invite the poor, the crippled, the lame, the blind, and you will be blessed" (LUKE 14:12–14).

He told a parable of the prodigal son who demanded his inheritance early and then squandered it on prostitutes and riotous living (SEE LUKE 15:11–31).

"The love of money is the root of all evil" (I TIM. 6:10 KJV). *That's why Jesus issues more warnings about materialism and wealth than any other sin. Obviously, it takes a steady hand to hold a full cup.*

Jesus said to His disciples, "No servant can serve two masters. Either he will hate the one and love the other, or he will be devoted to the one and despise the other. You cannot serve both God and Money" (LUKE 16:13).

He told a parable of the rich man who had everything. The man was clothed in fine purple and linen, and he ate the very best food. But he was unconcerned about the misery of the beggar Lazarus, who was hungry and covered with sores. The rich man died and went to hell where he was tormented, but Lazarus was taken to heaven where he was comforted (SEE LUKE 16:19–31).

He spoke to a rich young ruler and commanded him to sell all he had and give it to the poor. The man went away very sorrowfully "because he was a man of great wealth" (LUKE 18:18–23).

Finally, Jesus turned to His disciples and said, "How hard it is for the rich to enter the kingdom of God!

Indeed, it is easier for a camel to go through the eye of a needle than for a rich man to enter the kingdom of God" (LUKE 18:24).

Isn't it incredible how many of Jesus' statements dealt with money in one way or another? We must ask ourselves why. Is there a reason the Master kept returning to that theme? Of course there is. Jesus was teaching us that great spiritual danger accompanies the pursuit and the achievement of wealth. He explained why in Matthew 6:21, "For where your treasure is, there your heart will be also."

GIVE THE LORD FIRST PLACE

The Lord will not settle for second place in your life. That is the threat posed by money. It can become our treasure—our passion—our greatest love. And when that happens, God becomes almost irrelevant.

Now, what does this understanding mean in today's world? Are we prohibited from earning a living, owning a home and car, having a savings account? Certainly not. In fact, we read in 1 Timothy 5:8, "If anyone does not provide for his relatives, and especially for his immediate family, he has denied the faith and is worse than an unbeliever." Men, specifically, are required to provide for and protect their families, which requires them to bring in money from their labors.

Wealth is not an evil in itself, either. Abraham, David, and other great men of the Bible were blessed with riches. And in fact, the Scriptures indicate that God gives to some people the power to get wealth (SEE DEUT. 8:18 AND 1 SAM. 2:7). Then where is the point of danger? The apostle Paul clarified for us that money is not the problem. It is the love of money that is the root of all evil (SEE 1 TIM. 6:10). We get into trouble when our possessions become a god to us.

What, then, is the biblical approach to possessions and money? We've seen what is wrong, but what is right? According to Christian financial counselor and author Ron Blue, there are four principles for money management that are foundational. If they are implemented in your life, you'll never have a problem with materialism. Let's look at them quickly:

PRINCIPLE 1: GOD OWNS IT ALL.

Some people have the notion that the Lord is entitled to 10 percent of our income, which is called our "tithes," and that the other 90 percent belongs to us. Not true. I believe strongly in the concept of tithing, but not because God's portion is limited to a tenth. We are but stewards of all that He has entrusted to us. He is our possessor—and sometimes our dispossessor. Everything we have is but a loan from Him. When God took away his wealth, Job had the correct attitude, saying, "Naked

I came from my mother's womb, and naked I will depart. The LORD gave and the LORD has taken away; may the name of the LORD be praised" (JOB 1:21).

If you understand this basic concept, it becomes clear that every spending decision is a spiritual decision. Waste, for example, is not a squandering of our resources. It is a poor use of His.

Expenditures for worthwhile purposes, such as vacations, ice cream, bicycles, blue jeans, magazines, tennis rackets, cars, and hamburgers, are also purchased with His money. That's why in my family, we bow to thank the Lord before eating each meal. Everything, including our food, is a gift from His hand.

PRINCIPLE 2: THERE IS ALWAYS A TRADE-OFF BETWEEN TIME AND EFFORT AND MONEY AND REWARDS.

You've heard the phrases "There's no such thing as a free lunch" and "You can't get something for nothing." Those are very important understandings. Money should always be thought of as linked to work and the sweat of our brow.

Here's how this second principle has meaning for us. Think for a moment of the most worthless, unnecessary purchase you have made in recent years. Perhaps it was an electric shaver that now sits in the garage, or an article of clothing that will never be worn. It is important to realize that this item was not purchased with your money; it was bought with your time, which you traded for money. In effect, you swapped a certain proportion of your allotted days on earth for that piece of junk that now clutters your home.

When you understand that everything you buy is purchased with a portion of your life, it should make you more careful with the use of money.

PRINCIPLE 3: THERE IS NO SUCH THING AS AN INDEPENDENT FINANCIAL DECISION.

There will never be enough money for everything you'd like to buy or do. Even billionaires have some limitations on their purchasing power. Therefore, every expenditure has implications for other things you need or want. It's all linked together. What this means is that those who can't resist blowing their money for junk are limiting themselves in areas of greater need or interest.

And by the way, husbands and wives often fight over the use of money. Why? Because their value systems differ and they often disagree on what is wasteful. My mother and father were typical in this regard. If Dad spent five dollars for shotgun shells or for tennis balls,

he justified the expenditure because it brought him pleasure. But if Mom bought a five-dollar potato peeler that wouldn't work, he considered that wasteful. Never mind the fact that she enjoyed shopping as much as he did hunting or playing tennis. Their perspectives were simply unique. This is a potential problem you and your future spouse will just have to work through.

Again, this third principle involves a recognition that an extravagance at one point will eventually lead to frustration at another point. Good business managers are able to keep the big picture in mind as they make their financial decisions.

PRINCIPLE 4: DELAYED GRATIFICATION IS THE KEY TO FINANCIAL MATURITY.

Since we have limited resources and unlimited choices, the only way to get ahead financially is to deny ourselves some of the things we want. If we don't have the discipline to do that, then we will always be in debt. Remember, too, that unless you spend less than you earn, no amount of income will be enough. That's why some people receive salary increases and soon find themselves even deeper in debt.

Let me repeat that important concept: No amount of income will be sufficient if spending is not brought under control. Consider the finances of the United States government, for example. It extracts more than a trillion dollars annually from American taxpayers. That's a thousand billion bucks! But our Congress spends hundreds of billions more than that.

Even by the most liberal interpretation, much of this revenue is wasted on programs that don't work and on unnecessary and expensive bureaucracies. Consequently, the size of our national debt is mind-boggling. The point is inescapable: Whether it be within a government or by a private individual, there must be a willingness to deny short-term gratification and to live within one's means. It isn't easy, but it pays big dividends at maturity.

Well, maybe these four principles will help you build a foundation of financial stability without compromising your belief system. In short, the secret of successful living is to spend your life on something that will outlast it, or, as the writer to the Hebrews said, "Keep your lives free from the love of money and be content with what you have" (HEB. 13:5).

THE POWERBROKERS

Let's return to the question with which we began: What goals are worthy of the investment of your life? We haven't answered it

No amount of income will be sufficient if spending is not brought under control.

definitively, but we've eliminated money as a worthy objective. Now we will look at another driving force that is even more influential in shaping the way things work. I'm referring to the pursuit of power. The lust for it permeates human societies and has its origins very early in life.

Most of us want to run things. Even the desire for money we just discussed is a function of this longing for control and influence. Why? Because those with the most money are perceived as being the most powerful.

Just how important is raw power in your own motivational system? Will it shape your choice of a career? Do you hope to be a doctor, lawyer, military officer, or politician because these professions represent influence in the culture? Are you determined to make a name for yourself? Do you want people to say when you pass, "There goes a great person"? Do you hope they'll want your autograph and your photograph? Is your purpose in living to be found in these symbols of significance?

If so, your ladder is leaning against the wrong wall. But let me hasten to clarify. God has given you talent, and He wants you to use it productively. You should set your goals high and direct your energies toward achieving them. Train your mind. Develop your skills. Discipline your appetites. Prepare for the future. Work hard. Go for it! You can't steal second with one foot on first.

The lust for power permeates human societies and has its origins very early in life.

But before you set out to make your mark, you should ask yourself, "For whom will this be done?" If you seek power so you can be powerful, you're on the wrong track. If you crave fame so you can be famous, the journey will be disappointing. If you desire influence so you can be influential, you're making a big mistake. This is what the Lord says about these trappings of success: "Let not the wise man glory in his wisdom, neither let the mighty man glory in his might, let not the rich man glory in his riches" (JER. 9:23 KJV). What, then, should we glory in? The apostle Paul provides the answer: "So whether you eat or drink or whatever you do, do it all for the glory of God" (1 COR. 10:31).

That's very clear, isn't it? Our purposes are not our own. They are His. Thus, the choice of an occupation and "whatever you do" is to be motivated by your service to the kingdom of God. That is the only thing that carries eternal significance. Nothing else will satisfy.

Everything else is going to burn.

I have lived long enough to see some of my early dreams of glory come unstitched. One of them began shortly after I graduated from high school and went off to college. I arrived on campus several days before classes started and walked around looking at the place that would be my home for the next four years. I was like a tourist on holiday.

Of greatest interest to me that morning was the trophy case standing in the main administration building. There behind the glass were the glitzy symbols of past athletic victories. Basketball, track, and baseball were well represented there. Then I saw it. Standing majestically at the

Those with the most money are perceived as being the most powerful.

center of the case was the perpetual tennis trophy. It was about two feet tall and had a shiny little man on top. Engraved on the shaft were the names of all the collegiate tennis champions back to 1947. Every one of those heroes was burned into my memory. I could name most of them today.

As I stood there before that historic trophy, I said to myself, "Someday! Some fine day I'm going to add my name to that list of legends." I set my jaw and determined to show the world.

As strange as it may seem today, becoming our college tennis champ was my highest goal in living at that time. Nothing could have mattered more to me. Tennis had been my passion in high school. I had played six days a week and eleven months per year. When I graduated and headed for college, it was with the intention of riding this sport into the record books.

Well, I did have a certain amount of success with my tennis career. I lettered all four years, captained the team as a senior, and yes, I got my name inscribed on the big trophy. In fact, I did it twice during each of my last two seasons. I left the college with the satisfaction of knowing that future generations of freshmen would stand at the display case and read my name in admiration. Someday they might be great like me.

WHERE'S THAT TROPHY NOW?

Alas, about fifteen years later a friend had reason to visit the college I attended. He was dumping something in the trash behind the administration building, and what do you suppose he found? Yep, there among the garbage and debris was the perpetual tennis trophy!

The athletic department had actually thrown it away! What a blow! There I was, a legend in my own time, and who cared? Some universities retire the jersey numbers of their greatest athletes. My school didn't retire my number. They retired my memory!

The friend, Dr. Wil Spaite, who had been one of my teammates in college, took the tennis trophy home and cleaned it up. He put a new shiny man on the top and bought a new base for it. Then he gave it to me to commemorate our "prime," which everyone appeared to have forgotten. That trophy stands in my office today. I'll show it to you if you come by for a visit. My name is on it twice. You'll be impressed. It was a big deal at the time. Honest.

This brief encounter with fame has taught me a valuable lesson about success and achievement. Pay attention now, because this could be on the midterm: IF YOU

LIVE LONG ENOUGH, LIFE WILL TRASH YOUR
TROPHIES, TOO. I don't care how important something seems at the time, if it is an end in itself, the
passage of time will render it old and tarnished. Who
cares today that Zachary Taylor or William Henry
Harrison won their elections for president of the
United States? Can you name three U.S. senators in the
year 1933? Probably not, and who cares anyway? What
difference did it make that the Brooklyn Dodgers
defeated the Yankees in the 1955 World Series? The
hero of that series, Sandy Amoros, made a game-saving
catch that a nation cheered, but he was soon penniless,
forgotten, and living on the streets.

SUCCESS, TOO, WILL FADE

That's the way the system works. Your successes will fade
from memory, too. That doesn't mean you shouldn't try
to achieve them. But it should lead you to ask, "Why
are they important to me? Are my trophies for me, or

are they for Him?" Those are critical questions that every believer is obligated to answer.

We've seen that the desire for influence and control is basic to the human personality, especially among men. But how much satisfaction does it bring to those who achieve it? I would not deny that authority is intoxicating for some people and that they crave the perks that go with it. Nevertheless, power is at best a temporary phenomenon that eventually must be surrendered.

If the triumphs of the world's superstars and power-brokers so quickly turn to dust, how much less significant will be the modest achievements you and I will be likely to garner? If our successes are simply ends in themselves, are they worth the investment of our years? Do they justify our brief tenure on this mortal soil? Is that all there is to a fire? I believe most passionately that it is not!

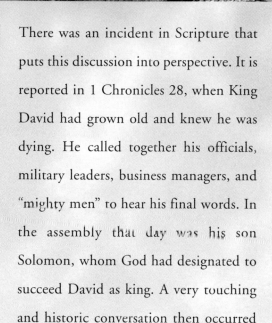

There was an incident in Scripture that puts this discussion into perspective. It is reported in 1 Chronicles 28, when King David had grown old and knew he was dying. He called together his officials, military leaders, business managers, and "mighty men" to hear his final words. In the assembly that day was his son Solomon, whom God had designated to succeed David as king. A very touching and historic conversation then occurred between the dying monarch and his young heir.

Power is a temporary phenomenon that must be surrendered.

SOUND ADVICE FROM A DYING KING

The advice David gave that day was of great significance, not only for Solomon but also for you and me. A person doesn't waste words when the death angel hovers nearby. Picture the scene, then, as the old man offers his last thoughts to his beloved son who would carry on his legacy. This is what David said, probably with strong feeling and a shaky voice:

> And thou, Solomon my son, know thou the God of thy father, and serve him with a perfect heart and with a willing mind: for the LORD searcheth all hearts, and understandeth all the imaginations of the thoughts: if thou seek him, he will be found of thee; but if thou forsake him, he will cast thee off for ever. (1 CHRON. 28:9 KJV)

A lifetime of wisdom was packed into that brief statement from the godly king. Notice first that David advised Solomon to "know" God. He didn't say "know about God." I know about Abraham Lincoln, but I never met him. David wanted Solomon to be acquainted personally with the God of Israel, whom he had tried to serve with a willing mind.

Then the king laid before his son the fundamental issue facing every person who ever lived. He said, "If thou seek him, he will be found of thee; but if thou forsake him, he will cast thee off for ever." If I had a thousand years to consider a final message for my son or daughter, I couldn't improve on these last words of David.

It is also my best advice to you as we conclude this discussion of purposes and goals. Whatever else you set out to do, begin by getting to know God and seeking His will in your life. If you do that, you will find Him. He will lead you. He

Whatever you set out to do, begin by getting to know God and seeking His will.

will bless you. What a wonderful promise! But it is conditional. If you turn your back on the Lord, He will cast you off forever. I owe it to you, the reader, to emphasize that sobering warning as well.

How interesting it is that the young prince who heard his father's advice on that day went on to become perhaps the richest, most famous, and most glamorous king in the history of the world. He received twenty-five tons of gold every year (at today's value that is $308 million) and every form of wealth to go with it. The Scripture says, "King Solomon was greater in riches and wisdom than all the other kings of the earth. The whole world sought audience with Solomon to hear the wisdom God had put in his heart. Year after year, everyone who came brought a gift—articles of silver and gold, robes, weapons and spices, and horses and mules.... As Solomon grew old, his wives turned his heart after other gods, and his heart was not fully devoted to the LORD his God, as the heart of David his father had been. He followed Ashtoreth the goddess of the Sidonians, and Molech the detestable god of the Ammonites. So Solomon did evil in the eyes of the LORD; he did not follow the LORD completely, as David his father had done" (1 KINGS 10:23–25; 11:4–6).

Solomon had lost all meaning in life, which explains his boredom with riches, fame, women, slaves, accomplishments, gold, and even laughter. God's hand was no longer on him.

The lesson for the rest of us is clear. If we ignore the Lord and violate His commandments, there will be no meaning for us, either. The temporal things of this world, even vast riches and power, will not deliver the satisfaction they advertise! There must be something more substantial on which to base one's values, purposes, and goals. And of course there is. Jesus said it succinctly: "*But seek ye first the kingdom of God, and his righteousness;* and all these things shall be added unto you" (MATT. 6:33 KJV, emphasis mine).

I rest my case.

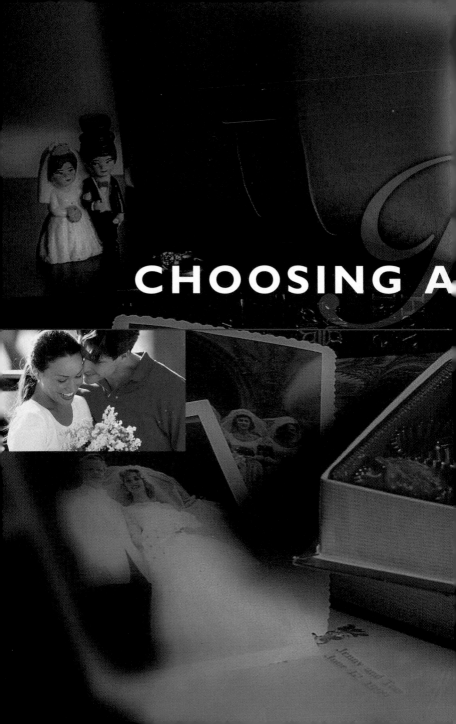

CHOOSING A

PARTNER

We're going to turn a hard corner now and talk briefly about another life-changing issue you will probably deal with during the critical decade. It concerns the choice of a marriage partner and the establishment of a family. Not everyone will decide to marry, of course, but approximately 77 percent of you will make that move sooner or later.

The tragedy of modern families is how frequently they break up. No one knows for sure what the probabilities of divorce are, but they are far too high. (We hear often that 50 percent of marriages end in divorce, but that estimate is based on faulty information.) What we do know for certain is that marriage is a risky enterprise that must be entered into with great care. It can result either in lifelong companionship or some of the most bitter experiences in living.

Make no mistake about it, divorce inflicts terrible pain on its victims. Every member of the family suffers when a marriage blows up. A Russian woman who was my guest on the radio talked about her years in a Nazi extermination camp. She had seen mass murder and every form of deprivation. After the war, she came to America and married, only to have her husband be unfaithful and abandon her a few years later. Unbelievably, she said that experience of rejection and loss was actually more painful than her years in a German death camp. That says it all.

If husbands and wives suffer dramatically from the breakup of their families, imagine how much more painful it is for their vulnerable children. Some of you have reason to understand precisely what I mean because you've been there. It is not a pretty picture. Research focusing on children of divorce shows that emotional security in children is dependent on the presence of a warm, nurturing, sustained, and continuous interaction with both parents. When those relationships are interrupted, some kids never fully recover from it. In fact, one study showed that 90 percent of children from divorced homes suffered from an acute sense of

Marriage is a risky enterprise: It can result in either lifelong companionship or some of the most bitter experiences in life.

shock, including profound grieving and irrational fears. Fifty percent reported feeling rejected and abandoned, and for good reason. Half the fathers never came to see their children three years after the divorce. Most significantly, 37 percent of the children were even more unhappy and dissatisfied five years after the divorce than they had been at eighteen months. In other words, time did not heal their wounds.

FOR THOSE OF YOU
WHO PLAN TO MARRY

To my readers who plan to marry, I urge you to be extremely careful in the selection of a mate. Bathe the matter in prayer, and bring all of your intelligence to bear on the decision. You do not want this tragedy of divorce to happen to you. It must not happen to you.

Unfortunately, many young people are not so cautious. They move glibly through their courtship and into marriage, not seeming to realize just how much is at stake for them. They remind me of a candy lover peering into a box of delicious chocolates. He has been offered only one piece, and the decision is killing him. There are too many choices. Some are creams, some contain nuts, some are fruit-filled, and some are chewy nougats. The guy's mouth waters for a particular chocolate, but where is it? In frustration, he begins crushing the tops to see what's inside of them. Finally, he bites into the one he has chosen. If he makes a mistake, he will know it instantly. But by then, it is too late. The box is passed to someone else.

Haven't you seen young men and women looking intently for the "perfect" chocolate? They know what they want but aren't sure how to find it. Furthermore, the decoration on the outside is often misleading. Their search leads them to crush many potential lovers along the way. At last, they "bite" into the chosen delicacy, only to realize very quickly that they should have given the matter a little more thought.

The big question is, How will you select the right chocolate from all the alternatives? How will you avoid a sour surprise after it is too late to reconsider? How will you beat the odds against a successful marriage? How will you prevent the fever of infatuation from turning into a marital rash? What are the principles that undergird a relationship and give it the very best chance of growing and maturing and surviving?

Those questions have been examined carefully by a researcher named Desmond Morris. His findings should be very enlightening to you. Dr. Morris wanted to understand why some couples develop a mystical union that holds them together for a lifetime while others fall apart when the pressure is on. The investigation began.

Dr. Morris soon recognized that the difference between successful and unsuccessful marriages can often be traced to how well couples are able to "bond" during the courtship period. By bonding he referred to the process by which a man and woman become cemented together emotionally. It describes the chemistry that permits two previous strangers to become intensely valuable to one another. It helps them weather the storms of life and remain committed in sickness and health, for richer or poorer, for better or

The overwhelming feeling of being "in love" is not a very reliable emotion during the early years (or at any age!). This intense affection can evaporate in a matter of days, leaving the person confused (and perhaps unhappily married). The only way to know you are in love with another person is to give yourselves plenty of time to get acquainted. Once the decision is made to marry, then your commitment to one another will be much more important than your feelings, which are certain to come and go.

worse, forsaking all others until they are parted in death. It is a phenomenal experience that almost defies description.

SOMEONE ON YOUR TEAM

Instead of being alone, a person's basic need for love, belonging, and acceptance is met in that precious relationship. If it has happened to you, there is now someone on your team who is looking out for your welfare. This person is fighting for you and defending you and praying for you. It's someone who will be there when things go wrong. He or she will also share your hopes and dreams and joy. And if your union should be blessed with children, this person will help you raise them in the fear and admonition of the Lord.

This special bonding is God's gift of companionship to the human family. It all started in the Garden of Eden when the first man, Adam, showed evidence of great loneliness. Can't you see him sitting on a log in the middle of the garden, drawing little circles in the sand with his toe? His eyes are glassy, and he yawns absent-mindedly. The Creator looks at Adam compassionately and says, "It is not good for the man to be alone" (GEN. 2:18). Imagine that! Even though Adam could fellowship with God Himself in the cool of the day, he needed something else. He needed human companionship. So the Father said, "I will make a helper suitable for him" (GEN. 2:18).

That word *suitable* in this Scripture is one of the Lord's profound understatements! He beautifully designed the sexes for one another, giving each gender the precise characteristics needed by the other. Consider, for example, how men's and women's bodies were crafted to "fit" together sexually. Anyone, even the most avid evolutionist, can see that they were constructed anatomically for one another. In the same way, the emotional apparatus of males and females is designed to interlock. It fits like hand in glove. Having thus prepared us lovingly for one another, the Lord revealed His plan for the family: "'For this reason a man will leave his father and mother and be united to his wife, and the two will become one flesh.' So they are no longer two, but one. Therefore what God has joined together, let man not separate" (MARK 10:7–9).

That is the way the system was designed. Unfortunately, there is a flaw in its implementation. Sin has invaded God's creation, and we live now in a fallen world. God's beautiful plan has been corrupted by selfishness, lust, greed, jealousy, suspicion, adultery, immaturity, and other distortions of the human personality. Consequently, romantic love sometimes fails to deliver on its promise, even among God-fearing people. Someone observed, "Marriages are made in heaven, but so are lightning and thunder."

WILL YOU EXPERIENCE
TRUE INTIMACY?

Studies have shown that only 10 percent of couples ever experience true intimacy in their relationship. Others may remain together for the sake of the children or from a sense of duty or because they genuinely care about each other. But they never achieve the companionship and affection they desire and need.

In that kind of imperfect world, let me ask you again about your own future. How will you secure the prize of intimacy in marriage? What are the keys to a deeply committed and satisfying relationship? How will you go the distance when others within your generation are breaking up every day? Is there a way to improve your prospects for marital happiness?

For the answers, let's review the findings of Dr. Morris. He said the quality of the bond made during courtship is the key to successful marriages. Then he explained how that cementing process occurs. Dr. Morris believes, and I strongly agree, that couples are most likely to bond securely when they have not rushed the dating experience. Time is the critical ingredient.

That reminds me of my efforts to build model airplanes when I was a boy. In those days, one could buy inexpensive kits that included a sheet of balsa wood on which the parts of the model had been stamped. It was a big chore to cut them with an Exacto knife and then glue all the pieces together. Once that was finished, tissue paper was pasted to the frame. The final result was a beautiful little plane to hang in your bedroom. I wanted to build one of those models in the worst way, but I never got it done. Repeatedly, I bought a kit and began cutting out the pieces. But I couldn't finish the project because I was too impatient to wait for the glue to dry. I wouldn't leave the fuselage alone, and it would fall apart in my hands.

That's more or less what Dr. Morris has told us about romantic relationships. It takes time for the glue to dry. A proper bond between two people is severely damaged if the process is rushed. Specifically, he said there are twelve stages of intimacy through which couples should progress if they want to develop a permanent commitment to each other. These stages begin with the most casual contact and move through categories of increasing familiarity.

Bonding is damaged when couples scramble the stages. If they kiss passionately on the first date, engage in heavy petting a month later, or have sexual intercourse before marriage, something precious is lost in their commitment to one another. They have not allowed the "glue" to dry. Unfortunately, that's how the entertainment industry presents the ideal romantic relationship. A young man and woman are shown being introduced, and the next thing you know, they're making passionate

STAGE ONE:	_Eye to Body_
STAGE TWO:	_Eye to Eye_
STAGE THREE:	_Voice to Voice_
STAGE FOUR:	_Hand to Hand_
STAGE FIVE:	_Hand to Shoulder_
STAGE SIX:	_Hand to Waist_
STAGE SEVEN:	_Face to Face_
STAGE EIGHT:	_Hand to Head_
STAGE NINE:	_Hand to Body_
STAGE TEN:	_Mouth to Breast_
STAGE ELEVEN:	_Touching Below the Waist_
STAGE TWELVE:	_Sexual Intercourse_

love together. According to Dr. Morris, that exploitation for momentary pleasure carries serious implications for the future of the relationship.

When the various stages are taken slowly and in order, two people have a chance to become knowledgeable of each other on an emotional, as opposed to a physical, level. Their courtship is nurtured through leisurely walks and talks and "lover's secrets" that lay a foundation for mutual intimacy. They talk endlessly about anything and everything. And by the time they marry, there is very little they don't know about each other. Romantic commitments are born in those prolonged conversations.

SUGGESTIONS TO HELP YOU
FIND LIFELONG LOVE

Well, I could write a book on this subject—in fact, I already did. It's called *Love for a Lifetime*, and might be helpful to those who are contemplating marriage or are already newlyweds. At this point, I'll leave you with seven straightforward recommendations:

1. A Sunday school teacher gave me some advice when I was thirteen years of age that I never forgot. He said, "Don't marry the person you think you can live with. Marry the one you can't live without." There's great truth in this advice. Marriage can be difficult even when two people are passionately in love with one another. It is murder when they don't have that foundation to build on.

2. Don't marry someone who has characteristics that you feel are intolerable. You may plan to change him or

her in the future, but that probably won't happen. Behavior runs in deep channels that were cut during early childhood, and it is very difficult to alter them. In order to change a deeply ingrained pattern, you have to build a sturdy dam, dig another canal, and reroute the river in the new direction. That effort is rarely successful over the long haul.

Therefore, if you can't live with a characteristic that shows up during courtship, it may plague you for the rest of your life. For example, a person who drinks every night is not likely to give up that habit after the honeymoon. If he or she is foolish with money or is basically unclean or tends to get violent when irritated or is extremely selfish, these are red flags you should not ignore. What you see is what you get.

Of course, we all have flaws, and I'm not suggesting that a person has to be perfect to be a candidate for marriage. Rather, my point is that you have to decide if you can tolerate a quirky behavior for the rest of your life—because that's how long you may have to deal with it. If you can't, don't bank on deprogramming the partner after you've said "I do." I advise you to keep your eyes wide open before marriage and then half-closed thereafter.

3. Do not marry impulsively! I can think of no better way to mess up your life than to leap into this critical decision without careful thought and prayer. It takes time to get acquainted and to walk through the first eight steps of the bonding process. Remember that the dating relationship is designed to conceal information, not reveal it. Both partners put

Don't marry the person you think you can live with. Marry the one you can't live without.

The dating relationship is designed to conceal information, not reveal it.

on their best faces for the one they seek to attract. They guard the secrets that might be a turnoff. Therefore, many newlyweds get a big surprise during the first year of married life. I suggest that you take at least a year to get beyond the facade and into the inner character of the person.

4. If you are a deeply committed Christian, do not allow yourself to become "unequally yoked" with an unbeliever. You may expect to win your spouse to the Lord at some future date, and that does happen on occasion. But to count on it is risky at best, foolhardy at worst. Again, this is the question that must be answered: "Just how critical is it that my husband (or wife) shares my faith?" If it is essential and nonnegotiable,

as the Scripture tells us it should be for believers, then that matter should be given the highest priority in one's decision to marry.

5. Do not move in with a person before marriage. To do so is a bad idea for many reasons. First, it is immoral and a violation of God's law. Second, it undermines a relationship and often leads to divorce. Studies show that couples who live together before marriage have a 50 percent greater chance of divorce than those who don't, based on fifty years of data. Those who cohabit also have less satisfying and more unstable marriages. Why? The researchers found those who had lived together later regretted having "violated their moral standards" and "felt

Love at first sight is a physical and emotional impossibility. Why? Because love is much more than a romantic feeling. It is more than a sexual attraction or the thrill of the chase or a desire to marry someone. These are responses that can occur "at first sight," and they might even lead to the genuine thing in time. But those feelings are usually very temporary, and they do not mean the person who experiences them is "in love."

a loss of personal freedom to exit out the back door." Furthermore, and in keeping with the theme of marital bonding, they have "stolen" a level of intimacy that is not warranted at that point, nor has it been validated by the degree of commitment to one another. As it turns out, God's way is not only the right way—it is the healthiest for everyone concerned.

6. Don't get married too young. Making it as a family requires some characteristics that come with maturity, such as selflessness, stability, and self-control. It's best to wait for their arrival.

7. Finally, I'll conclude with the ultimate secret of lifelong love. Simply put, the stability of marriage is a by-product of an iron-willed determination to make it work. If you choose to marry, enter into that covenant with the resolve to remain committed to each other for life. Never threaten to leave your mate during angry

moments. Don't allow yourself to consider even the possibility of divorce. Calling it quits must not become an option for those who want to go the distance!

That was the attitude of my father when he married my mother in 1935. Forty years later, he and I were walking in a park and talking about the meaning of commitment between a husband and wife. With that, he reached in his pocket and took out a worn piece of paper. On it was written a promise he had made to my mother when she agreed to become his wife. This is what he had said to her:

> *I want you to understand and be*
> *fully aware of my feelings concerning*

If genuine love has escaped you thus far, don't begin believing "no one would ever want me." That is a deadly trap that can destroy you emotionally! Millions of people are looking for someone to love. The problem is finding one another!

Beware of blindness to obvious warning signs that tell you that your potential husband or wife is basically disloyal, hateful, spiritually uncommitted, hooked on drugs or alcohol, given to selfishness, etc. Believe me, a bad marriage is far worse than the most lonely instance of singleness.

the marriage covenant which we are about to enter. I have been taught at my mother's knee, and in harmony with the Word of God, that the marriage vows are inviolable, and by entering into them I am binding myself absolutely and for life. The idea of estrangement from you through divorce for any reason at all (although God allows one—infidelity) will never at any time be permitted to enter into my thinking. I'm not naive in this. On the contrary, I'm fully aware of the possibility, unlikely as it now appears, that mutual incompatibility or other unforeseen circumstances could result in extreme mental suffering. If such becomes the case, I am resolved for my part to *accept it as a consequence of the commitment I am now making, and to bear it, if necessary, to the end of our lives together.*

I have loved you dearly as a sweetheart and will continue to love you as my wife. But over and above that, I love you with a Christian love that demands that I never react in any way toward you that would jeopardize our prospects of entering heaven, which is the supreme objective of both our lives. And I pray that God Himself will make our affection for one another perfect and eternal.

If that is the way you approach the commitment of marriage, your probabilities of living happily together are vastly improved. Again, the Scripture endorses the permanence of the marital relationship: "Therefore what God has joined together, let man not separate" (MARK 10:9).

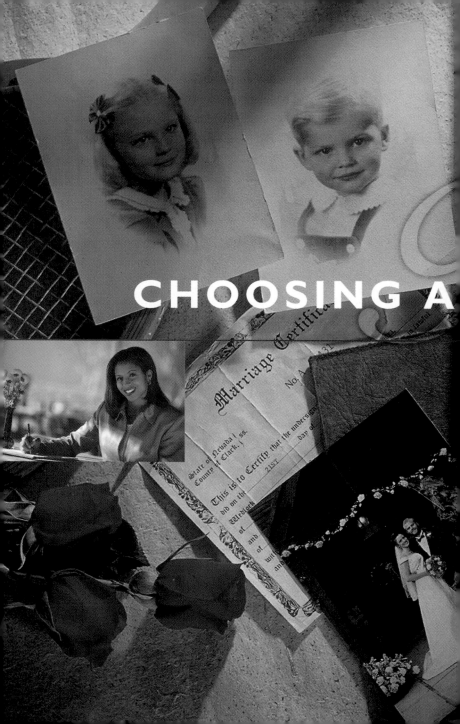

CHOOSING A

PURPOSE

One of my professional colleagues died toward the end of my final year on the staff of Children's Hospital of Los Angeles. He had served on our university medical faculty for more than twenty-five years. During his tenure as a professor, he had earned the respect and admiration of both professionals and patients, especially for his research findings and contribution to medical knowledge. This doctor had reached the pinnacle of success in his chosen field and enjoyed the status and financial rewards that accompany such accomplishment. He had tasted every good thing, at least by the standards of the world.

At the next staff meeting following his death, a five-minute eulogy was read by a member of his department. Then the chairman invited the entire staff to stand, as is our custom in situations of this nature, for one minute of silence in memory of the fallen colleague. I have no idea what the other members of the staff thought about during that sixty-second pause, but I can tell you what was going through my mind.

I was thinking, *Lord, is this what it all comes down to? We sweat and worry and labor to achieve a place in life, to impress our fellowmen with our competence. We take ourselves so seriously, overreacting to the insignificant events of each passing day. Then, finally, even for the brightest among us, all these successes fade into history and our lives are summarized with a five-minute eulogy and sixty seconds of silence. It hardly seems worth the effort, Lord.*

But I was also struck by the collective inadequacy of that faculty to deal with the questions raised by our friend's death. Where had he gone? Would he live again? Will we see him on the other side? Why was he born? Were his deeds observed and recorded by a loving God? Is that God interested in me? Is there a purpose to life beyond investigative research and professorships and expensive automobiles? The silent response by 250 learned men and women seemed to symbolize our inability to cope with those issues.

Well, how about it? Do you know where you stand on the fundamental issues posed by the death of my friend? More to the point, have you resolved them for yourself and for those you love? If not, then I hope you'll read on. We will devote this final chapter to those questions and to the search for life's ultimate meaning and purpose.

It is a matter of incredible significance. Until we know

who we are and why we are here, no amount of success, fame, money, or pleasure will provide much satisfaction. Until we get a fix on the "big picture," nothing will make much sense.

THE BREVITY OF LIFE

It might be useful to engage in a mental exercise I call the "end-of-life test." Project yourself many years down the road when your time on earth is drawing to a close. That may seem morbid to you at such a young age, but the brevity of life is a very important biblical concept. The psalmist David said our lives are like the flowers of the field that blossom in the morning and then fade away (SEE PS. 103:15–16). Moses expressed the same idea in Psalm 90 when he wrote, "Teach us to number our days" (V. 12 KJV). What the biblical writers were telling us is that we're just passing through. At best, we're merely short-termers on this planet.

Given this understanding of the brevity of life, I invite you to imagine yourself as an old man or woman looking back across many decades. Think about the highlights and treasures of the past seventy or eighty years. What kinds of memories will be the most precious to you in that final hour?

Ask yourself what you will care about when everything is on the line. Will it be the businesses you created and nourished? Will it be the plaques that hang on the wall? Will it be the academic degrees you earned from prestigious universities? Will it be the fortune you accumulated? Will it be the speeches you gave, the paintings you produced, or the songs you sang? Will it be the books you wrote or the offices to which you were elected? Will it be the power and influence you held? Will it be a five-minute eulogy and sixty seconds of silence after you're gone? I doubt it.

Achievements and the promise of posthumous acclaim will bring some satisfaction, no doubt. But your highest priorities will be drawn from another source. When all is said and done and the books are closing on your life, I believe your treasures will lie much closer to home. Your most precious memories will focus on those you loved, those who loved you, and what you did together in the service of the Lord. Those are the basics. Nothing else will survive the scrutiny of time.

To elaborate on that concept, let me take you to a gymnasium where my friends and I played basketball three times a week. On that particular morning, we had invited Pete Maravich to join us.

It was an audacious thing to do. "Pistol Pete," as he was dubbed by the media, had been one of the greatest basketball players of all times. He was the Michael Jordan or the Magic Johnson of his day. He set more than forty NCAA records at Louisiana State University, many of which still stand. He had averaged forty-four points per game during his three years at LSU. After graduation, Pete was drafted by the National Basketball Association and became the first player ever to receive a million-dollar contract.

What will you care about when everything is on the line… a five-minute eulogy and sixty seconds of silence after you're gone?

When he retired because of knee problems, he was elected to the NBA Hall of Fame the first year he was eligible. There is very little that can be done with a basketball that Pete Maravich didn't accomplish.

So for a bunch of "duffers" to invite a superstar like Pete to play with us took some gall, even though he was forty years old at the time. To our delight, he agreed to come and showed up at 7:00 A.M. I quickly learned that he had been suffering from an unidentified pain in his right shoulder for many months. Aside from playing in the NBA "Legends Game," which was televised nationally, Pete had not been on a basketball court in more than a year. Nevertheless, we had a good time that morning. Pete moved at about one-third his normal speed, and the rest of us huffed and puffed to keep up. We played for about forty-five minutes and then took a break to get a drink. Pete and I stayed on the court and talked while waiting for the other players to come back.

"You can't give up this game, Pete," I said. "It has meant too much to you through the years."

"You know, I've loved playing this morning," he replied. "I really do want to get back to this kind of recreational basketball. But it wouldn't have been possible in the last few months. The pain in my shoulder has been so intense that I couldn't have lifted a two-pound ball over my head."

"How are you feeling today?" I asked.

"I feel great," he said.

PETE'S LAST WORDS

Those were Pete's last words. I turned to walk away, and for some reason looked back in time to see him go down. His face and body hit the boards hard. Still, I thought he was teasing. Pete had a great sense of humor, and I assumed that he was playing off his final comment about feeling good.

I hurried over to where Pete lay and still expected him to get up laughing. But then I saw that he was having a seizure. I held his tongue to keep his air passage open and called for the other guys to come help me. The seizure lasted about twenty seconds, and then Pete stopped breathing. We started CPR immediately, but were never able to get another heartbeat or another breath. Pistol Pete Maravich, one of the world's greatest athletes, died there in my arms at forty years of age.

It is important to know something about Pete's background to understand who he was. Quite frankly, he had been a trouble-maker when he was younger. He was a heavy drinker who broke all the rules. His attitude deteriorated in the NBA, and he finally quit in a huff. This man who had received every acclaim that can come to an athlete hit the skids emotion-ally. After retirement, he stayed in his house day after day to avoid autograph-seeking fans and because he had nowhere to go. There he sat, depressed and angry, for two years.

Something incredible happened at that crucial moment in Pete's life. He was in bed one night when he heard someone speak his name. He sat upright, wonder-ing if he had been dreaming. Then he heard the voice again. Pete realized that

God was calling him. He immediately knelt beside his bed and gave his heart to the Lord. It was a total consecration of his mind, body, and soul.

For the last five years of his life, all he wanted to talk about was what Jesus Christ had done for him. He told that story to reporters, to coaches, to fans, and to anyone who would listen. The day Pete died, he was wearing a T-shirt that bore the inscription "Looking unto Jesus."

I was able to share that testimony with the media, which took it around the world within an hour. "You think Pete's great love was basketball," I told them, "but that was not his passion. All he really cared about was Jesus Christ and what He had done in Pete's life." And now I'm relaying that message to you. Perhaps that is why the Lord placed this good man in my arms as his life ebbed away.

HITTING CLOSE TO HOME

Now I need to tell you something highly personal that happened next. I went home and sat down with our son, Ryan, who was seventeen years old at the time. I asked to talk to him about something of extreme importance to us both.

I said, "Ryan, I want you to understand what has happened here. Pete's death was not an unusual tragedy that has happened to only one man and his family. We all must face death sooner or later and in one way or another. This is the 'human condition.' It comes too early for some people and too late for others. But no one will escape, ultimately. And, of course, it will also happen to you and me. So without being morbid about it, I want you to begin to prepare yourself for that time.

"Sooner or later, you'll get the kind of phone call that Mrs. Maravich received today. It could occur ten or

fifteen years from now, or it could come tomorrow. But when that time comes, there is one thought I want to leave with you. I don't know if I'll have an opportunity to give you my 'last words' then, so let me express them to you right now. Freeze-frame this moment in your mind, and hold on to it for the rest of your life. My message to you is Be there! Be there to meet your mother and me in heaven. We will be looking for you on that resurrection morning. Don't let anything deter you from keeping that appointment.

"Because I am fifty-one years old and you are only seventeen, as many as fifty years could pass from the time of my death to yours. That's a long time to remember. But you can be sure that I will be searching for you just inside the Eastern Gate. This is the only thing of real significance in your life. I care what you accomplish in the years to come, and I hope you make good use of the great potential the Lord has given to you. But above every other purpose and goal, the only thing that really matters is that you determine now to be there!"

That message is not only the most valuable legacy I could leave to Ryan and his sister, Danae. It is also the heart and soul of what I have tried to convey in this book. Be there! This must be our ultimate objective in living. Within that two-word phrase are answers to all the other questions we have posed.

Jesus Christ is the only satisfactory explanation for why we're here and where we're going.

Jesus Christ is the source—the only source—of meaning in life. He provides the only satisfactory explanation for why we're here and where we're going. Because of this good news, the final heartbeat for the Christian is not the mysterious conclusion to a meaningless existence. It is, rather, the grand beginning to a life that will never end.

That same Lord is waiting to embrace and forgive anyone who comes to Him in humility and repentance. He is calling your name, just as He called the name of Pete Maravich. His promise of eternal life offers the only hope for humanity. If you have never met this Jesus, I suggest that you seek spiritual counsel from a Christian leader who can offer guidance. You can also write to me, if that would help.

Thanks for reading along with me. I hope to meet you someday. If our paths don't cross this side of heaven, I'll be looking for you in that eternal city. By all means, *Be there!*

FOCUS ON THE FAMILY
8605 Explorer Drive
Colorado Springs, CO 80920